The Great Fire of London

Written by Hawys Morgan
Illustrated by Ludovic Salle

Collins

2 September 1666

It's one in the morning. A fire races up the walls of a bakery on Pudding Lane.

The baker and his family know they must take action. They wrench open a window and escape over the rooftops.

Church bells disturb the peace – something is wrong! People race along the streets, knocking loudly on doors. They shout wildly. Fire is **menacing** the city of London!

By six in the morning, the streets are full of confusion. Voices in **concerned** conversation say that three hundred houses burned down in the night. Now one hundred burn every hour!

3 September 1666

Fire leaps across the narrow spaces between the houses.

It climbs the walls as hot **embers** fall, burning the people below. Half the city is destroyed.

The **easterly** wind forces the fire onwards. It has not rained since last month, so the dry wooden houses catch fire easily. The combination of dry weather, wooden houses and wind means the city is blazing.

People quickly pack their possessions. They kneel in their gardens, hiding their treasures, like spices and expensive cheese, in pits.

Smoke circles people as they escape. They wrap fabric over their faces to protect themselves from the **toxic** smoke.

A huge **procession** of people clutch their possessions. Their only option is to leave the city.

4 September 1666

Fire wrecks the shops in Cheapside, making the paint wrinkle on the shop signs.

The king gives instructions to destroy everything in the fire's path to slow it down. Families glance sadly back at the destruction of their homes.

5 September 1666

The roads are so hot they burn people's feet.

At the riverside, there are hardly any boats left. People jump as the warehouses explode like bombs.

An angry red glow bounces off the water,
lighting up the castles and mansions of the city.

6 September 1666

On land, men's muscles ache as they use axes, fire hooks and leather buckets to bravely fight the fire. Even the king and his brother are helping!

The fire is finally under control, but most of the city has been destroyed.

The king is concerned about the many homeless people. The price of bread is very high. He orders that bread is handed out.

Many thousands of houses have been destroyed.
Over the coming months there will be discussions
about an improved design for the city.
London will never be the same again.

Timeline

2 September

The fire starts in Pudding Lane.

Hundreds of houses are burning every hour.

3 September

Half the city is destroyed.

4 Septembe

Houses are destroyed to stop the fire.

5 September

Most fires are put out.

6 September

Rubble is cleared and bread is given to the poor.

Glossary

concerned worried

easterly wind blowing from the east

embers small pieces of burning wood

menacing threatening to harm

procession a group of people walking

toxic bad for your health

Review: After reading

Use your assessment from hearing the children read to choose any GPCs, words or tricky words that need additional practice.

Read 1: Decoding

- Ask the children:
  - Look through the book. What words can you find with the /sh/ sound? (e.g. *action*, *conversation*, *combination*, *instructions*, *destruction*)

Read 2: Prosody

- Choose two double page spreads and model reading with expression to the children.
- Ask the children to have a go at reading the same pages with expression.
- Reading exclamation marks. Tell the children that exclamation marks show that a sentence is written with a specific feeling in mind. It could be excitement, worry, joy or another feeling.
- Model reading pages 3 and 4 to the children. When you read the sentences ending with exclamation marks use expression to make the feeling of danger and sadness clear.
- Ask the children to read these sentences showing the feeling behind the exclamation mark.

Read 3: Comprehension

- Turn to pages 22 and 23. Discuss what happened on each day.
- For every question ask the children how they know the answer. Ask:
  - Where did the Great Fire of London start? (*a bakery in Pudding Lane*)
  - How did people escape? (*climbing over rooftops and in boats across the river*)
  - What was the king concerned about? (*the homeless people and the price of bread*)
  - Why do you think people buried their treasure in their gardens? (*to keep it safe*)